A–Z of Welsh Rugby

The A-Z of Welsh Rugby

Richard Rowe

y Lolfa

Thanks to Paul Baglow for advice with the book,
and special thanks to Naomi and Callum
for putting up with me.

Illustrations: Rebecca Kitchin

ISBN: 0 86243 948 5
ISBN-13: 978 0 86243 948 4

Printed on acid-free and partly recycled paper
and published and bound in Wales by
Y Lolfa Cyf., Talybont, Ceredigion SY24 5AP
e-mail ylolfa@ylolfa.com
website www.ylolfa.com
tel (01970) 832 304
fax 832 782

Foreword

We obviously don't know you personally, but whatever category shelf you picked this book from, we can guarantee we know that you're a rugby fan. Maybe you're wondering whether to buy this book because you're already £60 lighter in the pocket from buying the latest replica jersey. You don't know whether or not to save your cash, in case your mate can get you a match ticket – because you couldn't get one for the All Blacks game for love nor money… well, you could have done, but you didn't take advantage of the special ticket prices. Let's face it: who wants to watch Japan, Canada or the other teams making up the numbers in the autumn internationals?

Now, if any of the above applied to you, it means that rugby is probably in your blood. You were introduced to the God-given game at an early age. You probably picked up on the fact that on various Saturdays in February and March your dad, after a liquid breakfast, would disappear with random family members. There'd be a kiss for your Mam and off he'd go down the local rugby club. Sometimes they were lucky enough to actually be going to the game. Then of course he would kiss the ticket first, then Mam, and you'd spend the afternoon in front of *Grandstand* to see if you could see dad among a sea of red and white in the Taff end.

This encouraged you to start playing, and you weren't bad out there on the wing. Sometimes, if you were lucky, the fly-half and outside centre would pass – but only when they saw a big kid running at them with his teeth bared. But then, disaster struck! You lost your place to the boy in the other class who started shaving when he was 10 and had had a trial for Ponty Youth. So you and your mates used to play for the team in the park on Saturdays. Your sister's mates used to watch you and your career was going great – right up until that time you twisted your ankle in a rut down the rec. The doctor said it was a sprain but you knew that the ligaments had suffered irreparable damage and you had to admit to yourself that your playing days were over. The event on that fateful February day – when the park pitches should have been called off – put you in the former-player category. In short an expert analyst on every aspect of the game. You live and breathe rugby. You can name all of the players who touched the ball before Gareth Edwards' spectacular try against the Barbarians, you know the names of Kevin Bowring's kids and Gavin Henson's favourite make of fake tan. Furthermore, you know a damn sight more about the game than that Eddie Butler or Jonathan Davies.

And you don't need a video ref to see it was a try.

So you being a sociable and generous soul, you love to share your knowledge with anyone who will listen while there's a game on. If you wish to see the game you love, you have two options; you can squeeze in with the rest of the sardines on Arriva Trains and head for Queen Street station – amidst tuts from the shoppers who forgot there was a match on today – and then spend the entire game queuing outside a Cardiff pub. Or you can pop down to your local rugby club. A place where the Brains is cheap, the bar staff have local accents and the menu is a Clarksies or a bag of porky scratchings. The place is full of people you know – some you might even be related to, and this, by rights, gives you a captive audience. This is where your encyclopaedic knowledge of the game – from the brand of William Webb-Ellis' boots to why four pints of S.A. is always a better pre-match meal than Pasta Carbon Dioxide, or whatever it is they eat – will be released into the public domain. Oh yes, you know everything. Or do you? You'll think you know everything until you read this book.

The author has paid us a vast amount of money to say how fantastic this book is, but he needn't have bothered because it does exactly what it says on the tin. *The A-Z of Welsh Rugby* is a sideways look at the game, the good points and bad. It's funny, irreverent and on more than a few occasions, you will nod in agreement with what is between the covers. You see, Richard is still a player, and has spoken to many former players in order to write this book, but rather than pontificate on the game, he has actually listened, watched and absorbed everything surrounding it. So rather than listen to a bar-stool preacher, get your head in this book and you'll learn a lot more.

Chwarae teg!

Jase and Mel
Full Welsh Breakfast, Red Dragon Radio

Introduction

After buying this book, you might think you are going to be reading an intellectual book on Welsh rugby – and in some strange way it is. However, this book looks at the things that happen behind the scenes of this glamorous sport, more so with the fans and the stupid things that we get up to during the Welsh rugby season. It looks at the silly antics that both fans and players get up to on and off the rugby field, the jokes that the game involves, and what rugby means to Wales as a nation. It also looks at the social side of rugby in Wales, particularly at the going-away trips, and the fun that is associated with them.

Well, we've all been on rugby trips, haven't we? I know, being a Welsh rugby club player, I certainly have. Surely, it's part of the game. You play hard, tenacious rugby all year, on muddy, boggy pitches in winter, to sun-hardened pitches in spring. Then, after nearly eight months of broken bones and aching limbs, it is time for the end-of-season tour. Or it might just be a hard away game up in North Wales, which involves a bit of a drink and a sing-song afterwards. Tours are not always identical, though. Going on a tour is the time when everything starts to make sense. Forget the glory of winning the league and cup double. Forget the painful months of incessant physio on the aching hamstrings and pulled calves. In fact, forget everything, because it's tour time.

These tours usually take place in the warm month of May – more often than not, at the beginning. May Bank Holiday is a particular favourite for many Welsh rugby teams; you can almost taste the excitement and ebullience as this time of year approaches. The looks on the faces of the rugby players and the committee men are a joy to see as they get prepared for their annual tour – four days of pure relaxation. You can hear the talk in the village as the butcher converses with the baker.

"They deserve it though, Ken, they've had a bloody hard season."

"That's right, Dai. I've given them fifty pasties to take up with 'em. They'll probably be hungry on the way."

But it's not only the butcher and baker that think this. Even the wives and families of the Welsh tourists think they deserve a break. Conversation can be heard amongst the pegging of washing in the South Wales Valleys, as housewives natter over their garden fences.

"Ai, Dai's looking forward to the break. It'll do him good to have a few days' rest with the boys.

Tough old season this year."

"You're right, Glad, it'll do him a world of good."

A rest! A world of good! Do these people know what a rugby tour entails? Honestly, for those who have never experienced tour life, it is far from relaxing. I've been on a few, and I can honestly say that the word 'rest' is definitely not synonymous with the word 'tour', especially when one involves Welsh rugby boys. The irony behind these ridiculous thoughts lies within the fact that these rugby boys will need a rest when they come back – and these 'rests' normally last four weeks. By this time, the colour has returned to the tourists' faces and they can start eating food again.

So, now that I've grabbed your attention, I'm going to enlighten you on what this book is really about. For all those people who have never participated in tour life; for all those rookie tourists yet to experience tour life; and for all those naive, gullible wives and families who believe that tour time is a rest period, then just read on. It is not going to be a book full of lurid tales of debauchery and violence. Oh, no! Just look at it as an educational tool for any budding Welsh rugby club player who wants to know what Welsh rugby is really all about.

I spoke to many Welsh club members before I started writing this book, purely to get more of a feel of what rugby means to us Welsh. As a result, I have named the book *The A-Z of Welsh Rugby* . It has been called this for two reasons. First, because every letter will contain a story, and, second, because, out of a party of 38 tourists on one trip, only thirty-five could remember the alphabet. But this is not because these Welsh tourists were not erudite enough to know their A-Z; it simply lay with the fact that they were just too pissed to remember it.

I hope you enjoy reading the tales of drunkenness and silly rugby moments as much I did when writing them. We all know that rugby in Wales is so important to all of us. But, much more important than that, is the fact that we are so proud to be Welsh. We are proud that we live a country of beauty, a country that has character and pride. This is echoed in the words of the first verse of a poem, 'In Passing', written by Brian Harris in 1967:

> To be born in Wales,
> Not with a silver spoon in your mouth,
> But, with music in your blood
> And with poetry in your soul,
> Is a privilege indeed.

Enjoy!

A – Alcohol

Alcohol is a thing that everyone loves. It is a great relaxation medicine that fights against the everyday pressures of life, taking away the stresses and strains of work and living. Nearly everyone drinks alcohol. I would even go as far to say that 99.9 percent of us like it. Why wouldn't they? After all, it's fun and it brings out the confidence in us all. It does have its drawbacks: alcohol can make you do things you wouldn't normally do, and it can cause the worst headaches known to man. But, putting aside the bad things about alochol, at the end of the day, moderate drinking can be fun. It's as simple as that.

However, moderate drinking and rugby do not mix. It's either 12 pints or don't bother. In Welsh rugby, this is a must for any rugby player or fan. I am not sure why this is. Scientists have done years of research to try to work out why it is a requirement for rugby players to get competely hammered after a game. They have even tried to work out why someone who has never drunk a drop of alcohol all his life joins a rugby team and ends up a pisshead. So, if scientists cannot work it out, what hope do we Welsh rugby louts have?

That's the main reason why I've chosen alcohol. I won't try to go into it too much now; I'll just allow this first letter to be a little introduction into the world of Welsh rugby players and the drink, and why they go in hand-in-hand.

Many women sometimes wonder if their sons and husbands have a problem, when they watch their men stumble home on a Saturday night, slurring their words. With a curry in one hand, and a rugby progamme in the other, what more could any wife or mother ask for? Aren't they proud of their loved ones?

OK, some families do tend to worry their close relatives, by telling them stories about how drink can cause many problems in life; some young rugby boys even get taken in by this mendacity. While I was a young youth player, a story about someone dying from drink circulated around the rugby club. Inquisitve and slightly worried, I asked what had happened to him. With a smile as big as Rhymney, the club comedian said:

"Ai, he died from the drink. Terrible blow it was, There he was, clearing out his cellar, when a 22-gallon keg fell off the shelf. Terrible mess it was."

Being a totally naive youth player, I believed him, but I soon realised that it was all a joke.

It's like the time when my mother asked me if I had a problem with drink, because I kept falling over the kitchen mat every Saturday. With a grin on my face, in my drunken stupor, I looked up into her eyes and muttered,

"No, mam, I like it."

Alcohol – it does the funniest of things.

B – Bus Trips

Believe it or not, the bus journey can be a highlight of any trip or away game, where many a laugh and a joke have taken place. On the other hand, these journeys can be the total antithesis of laughter. These journeys always come at the end of a tour or a night out. There is no real point in elucidating why this is so. Just think of sleep deprivation, lack of food and vital vitamins and, of course, take into account the 100 pints of lager that almost every player has consumed, and you can get a clearer idea of why, on their return, the tourists resemble a army of skeletons.

For the letter B, however, I would rather concentrate on the funnier aspects than on the unhealthier ones.

This tale can be looked on as both funny and unhealthy, especially if you look at it from the view of a bus driver. Again, this story involves a rugby tour, and is about a team that plays its rugby in the valleys of South Wales. Some people, after hearing this story, believed it to be somewhat spurious, simply because of the surrealism associated with it.

It was quite a few years back, when this shenanigan occurred. Having been on quite a lively night out, the coach driver was on time as he waited for the drunken tour party to return. Despite the punctuality of the bus driver, he was quite a moany and cantankerous fella, and his name, funnily enough, was Ken. Earlier in the night, some of the nuttier of the tour party were concocting some sort of surprise for him, and, needless to say, when they returned to the bus that night, with a few too many drinkie winkies inside them, something was destined to happen.

For most of the journey back to the hotel, the driver seemed in quite a jocund mood; well, apparently, he had managed to smile at least once, but the Welsh boys put that down to wind. But this was not to last. When missiles began to be thrown around the bus, and the back doors had been opened, the driver started to get agitated: and, very soon, annoyed. It was the last straw for him, when one of the players threw a rugby ball at him, catching him sweetly in the back of the head.

Personally, I think that, if the driver had remained calm, then what happened next might never have occurred. But, due to the abrupt stopping of the bus and the psychotic shouting displayed on his behalf, the drunken tourists saw this as cheeky and decided to do something about it. This 'something' has been likened to kidnapping, some people have argued.

Because of his incessant shouting, the Welsh boys decided to take the driver to the back of the bus, to 'quieten him down'. Then, one of the older tourists took it upon himself to drive the bus home, totally forgetting his drunken state. Bear in mind, this was during the 1980s and drink driving wasn't as frowned upon as it is today. Nevertheless, the bus returned safely. Unfortunately, by the time it had reached its destination, there was no one there to drive it back to bus headquarters. The tour party left the scene and headed for their beds, while the driver, who was still shouting in a frenetic manner, was left tied to a lamppost, about fifteen miles away, his trousers around his ankles.

Rumour has it that, when the police came to his rescue, some hours after, he was still ranting and raving, and, for his troubles, he spent the rest of the morning behind bars.

He has never returned to bus driving since.

C – Conversations, funny sayings and all that...

Funny sayings usually spring from the mouths of many Welsh people. We cannot help it; it's just the way we are. But this doesn't really matter, because many people from different countries love our different, but extremely comical, sense of humour. Having done a bit of travelling myself, I've noticed that people from all over the world have a lot of time for the Welsh. It's strange to think back to the time when I was in Australia, and the natives asking me to 'speak a bit of Welsh'. It was completely ironic, because there I was, in one of the most beautiful countries in the world, and all their people wanted me to do was speak my home language. However, despite not being able to speak the lingo fluently, I did manage to convince them that Welsh was my first language. That was until the day when I came across a real Welsh speaker, who was living in Australia at the time. He caught me out on one occasion, however, when he overheard me telling some attractive women that they were beautiful. Thinking I was a young Welsh Romeo, the girls, obviously impressed by my apparent knowledge of the language, were obviously none the wiser that I was asking them where the nearest leisure centre was. Unfortunately for me, the real Welsh speaker overheard, and I was unveiled as the 'lying Welshman', who didn't know one sentence in Welsh.

So, writing this book has made me question why people like us so much. Thinking about this, I contemplated our personalities, and this has, once again, linked in nicely with Welsh rugby and the daftness that goes with it. As a result, I have choosen to write about the conversations and funny sayings that have existed in Welsh rugby over the years:

The Gareth Edwards speech:

This still makes me chuckle when I hear the story. I first heard of it a few years ago, when there was a documentary on the scrum-half. In it, Edwards remembers a Lions match, when he was nearly sent off for swearing at the referee. After reaching for his card, obviously ready to send Edwards off, the ref pulled Edwards over. Not wanting to leave the field, the Welsh scrum-half told the ref that he wasn't swearing at him, but talking to his captain in Welsh. Obviously very gullible, and not well-acquainted with the Welsh language, the ref let him off, only to find out later that the captain that day was Tom Kiernan of Ireland.

Other conversations have just been completely surreal. These can sometimes be heard between a coach and his players.

During one match, a young player called John had a little run-in with the manager before quite a serious match. The rain had been pelting down all week and it was touch and go whether the game would be on. The home side had been joking around in the changing rooms and the coach was becoming more and more agitated. John, who was in the manager's bad books anyway, for being late, was in typical mood as he participated in all the banter. The manager, on the other hand, wasn't in quite such a jocund mood as he came in the changing rooms, bellowing, "They're bouncing off the walls in there." What this really meant was that the away side was clearly up for the game. However, John took it as a joke and retorted, "What? It's slippery in there, is it?" with a smirk that lit up the changing room. This smirk soon faded though, as John was repeatedly hit by the angry manager. He obviously hadn't thought it was a joking moment.

This same manager was also involved in another comical conversation, and, to be honest, he took it as a joke. After giving a half-an-hour speech on drugs and how they are bad for you, he asked one of the newcomers if he believed in them. The boy in question was obviously picked on for a reason; because the manager did know about the boy's druggie friends. This didn't deter the youngster as he proudly answered, "Yeah, I believe in them. I've seen them," as the manager looked on with an incredulous stare.

Laughable stories like this are prominent in Welsh rugby. I've heard the most bizarre responses players make, when talking to their coaches. Before one match, a player was asked what he would do if someone was giving him a raking on the side of the ruck, and he seriously answered, "Take the rake off him." Another player, again new to rugby, was asked what position he preferred. Totally naïve to the question, the player answered, "From behind," much to the delight of the listening team members. This same player was none the wiser when he was further asked what boots he needed. Again, not thinking, he answered, "I'll need one for my left and one for my right." This time, though, he knew he'd said something stupid.

Other comical sayings have existed in other areas in rugby. These are just some of them:

On the training paddock: "C'mon 'en, boys. Pick a partner and line up in threes."

If a fellow rugby player has just come out of prison and you're waiting for the ball on the wing: "Inside, inside."

Playing touch rugby – First one to score: "C'mon 'en, boys – if no one scores, it'll be a winning try."

Sorting out a game of touch rugby: "Right, boys, we'll have to play 14-a-side because there's only 25 of us."

Half-Time Speech – a tired captain: "We've got this game tied up, boys. All we have to do to win is score more points than them."

A drunken chairman calling Iestyn Harris 'Justin' all night: "You know what, Just, you're the most famous celebrity we've had down this club."
Yeah – so famous, he doesn't even know Iestyn's name!

Steward talking to a drunken Welsh fan:
Steward: "Where are you gonna sit?"
Fan: "On my arse!"

Referee sending off a banned player:
Ref : "Right then, you're off. What's your name?"
Player to team mates: "What name did you tell me to give?"

Rugby player looking for a job:
Jobcentre person: "Are you any good with a hammer?"
Player: "Dunno, but I used to chuck the shot putt in school."

Same player in Jobcentre:
Jobcentre person: "Are you OK with heights?"
Player: "Yeah, great. I just don't like climbing ladders."

Same person in Jobcentre, before being ejected:
Jobcentre person: "We might have something lined up for you. Can you come in on Wednesday morning?"
Player: "I dunno. Think I'm working Wednesday."

You may well be laughing, but these are true stories. Every one of these funny sayings has come from the mouth of a rugby player, and these happen to be Welsh people. But that doesn't make us dull; it simply makes us different. And that's why we are loved wherever we go.

D – Digs

Where you stay whilst on rugby tours is something that doesn't creep into your mind before you go. All your brain can think about is what the nightlife will be like in the place where you are staying. This seems strange to me, when I think back to all the tours I've been involved in. Also, from talking to club members of other rugby clubs, to help me write this book, it seems that most of us have shared the same philosophy when it comes to choosing accommodation. Strictly speaking, if you were an English hotel owner, would you let a party of drunken Welsh boys stay in your hotel? No, you're probably thinking. And you're right, because I wouldn't either. Come to think of it, I wouldn't them sleep in my barn – if I had one.

So, why do these snobby, rich hotel proprietors do it? Is it because of the money? Is it because they think that Welsh rugby boys like to spend their time in the local opera house, or do they think they are going to have candle-lit dinners for forty-five in a posh restaurant? No. Then, let me tell you what it is. To ensure that your crazy rugby team has the best accommodation, you tell the hotel manager that you're from the local choir and that you are singing in a village not far from the hotel. On hearing this, the hotel manager doesn't hesitate to take the desposit; after all, a lot of money is to be made.

On arrival, there are a lot of puzzled faces as the Welsh tourists sing their way through the hotel doors. First, they cannot believe that they'll be staying in a five-star hotel, when they were told it would be a hostel with fifteen to a room, and, second, the manager and his staff cannot believe their eyes, when they watch forty drunken Welsh tourists singing in the foyer. The manager can recognise immediately that the whole choir thing is a lie, after hearing the cacophonous din the boys make on entrance; and the fact that they have *Welsh Rugby Boys on Tour* emblazoned on their T-shirts almost gives it away.

Sometimes the ironic thing is, that even though a lot of money has been paid for them to stay at the hotel, usually, not all the rooms are taken. The guarantee is that there'll be at least 12 boys staying in the same room – just to have a late-night drink, and there'll always be a few more, either sleeping in the corridor, or sleeping in the bushes outside the hotel. Therefore, what the tour organiser should explain to the hotel manager is that all the club will be needing are four rooms, one corridor and a few bushes, for three nights. That way, the club saves money.

This is the reason that I've put 'Digs' in for the letter D – so if any other Welsh rugby tourists are told they're spending four days of their tour on a park bench, they will be in for one hell of a surprise. It'll proabably be the Hilton!

E – Entertainment

For those involved in rugby, every club has an entertainer, someone who you can guarantee will make people laugh. You must have. It's the Welsh rugby way of life.

In Welsh rugby, entertainment is everywhere, and this wacky entertainment usually happens whilst touring. From the minute you step on that coach, you know you are in for a laugh. As the bus doors open, you cannot help but smile as you see the driver sitting there with a face like thunder. You find it funny because you are going on a tour for 4 days, and the driver has to drive you everywhere. No disrespect to bus drivers, but I couldn't do it for two reasons. First, I couldn't drive anywhere, when 45 rugby boys are drinking and singing behind me; and, second, I haven't got my bus-driving licence.

But tours are great fun. The entertainment factor is second to none. And the greatest thing about them is that people think they can do what they want. They think, because they're on tour, they can get away with things they wouldn't normally get away with. And, ironically, this is normally the case.

For instance, the bus stops at the service station. The party of tourists gets out, slightly half-cut, and starts singing outside the services. But, strangely, no-one says anything. Security guards laugh as they watch the tour party sing the second verse of 'Working Man', and old women stop and take photos to put on their mantelpieces back home. It is utter madness; sometimes, I swear, half these people do not realise that it's only 10 o'clock in the morning. Then, just to make the scene more surreal and entertaining, you have the entertainer of the group pretending he is a butcher, pretending to sell legs of lamb to the bemused onlookers. It's one of those: 'you have to be there'.

And, in the services it's worse. Because the rugby boys know they're over the bridge and in England, they think they don't have to pay for anything. They walk into the shops and walk back out with a handfuls of stuff. Sometimes, it seems that they don't realise they're doing it.

When it's time to leave, the scene seems even more dream-like, with the busload of tourists having a goodbye wave from the people who are in the services. The boys love it. Either that, or they're sniggering at the dirty magazines they've just pilfered from the store. This entertainment lasts all tour. The tourists love the fact that they are free to do what they want. Four days' freedom with the boys. Now that's entertainment!

Entertainment can have a totally different context. This next tale was entertaining for a lot of people, apart from the boy in question, because he happened to miss one of the best, and most memorable, games ever – and that's why it's in this book.

Wales against England – the opening game of the Six Nations during Grand Slam year – 2005. What more could any budding Welsh rugby fan want? What's more, a ticket in one of the best seats in the Millennium Stadium. Can things get any better? Not even Willy Wonka could provide as much. But this Welsh fan didn't have to rip open thousands of chocolate bars like Charlie Bucket to get his ticket. No, the lucky bugger won it down his local rugby club. It is quite tough to get tickets for Welsh matches anyway, but when it's Wales against the most loathed rugby side in the world, it's even harder. However, this boy had one.

Going down to the game that day, the rugby fan's face gleamed with pleasure as he sat on the Rhymney Valley train. Seated with his mates, all of whom had paid for a ticket, and were fortunate to get one – the atmosphere on the train was electrifying as everyone awaited the big match.

Cardiff was heaving, when they got into Queen Street, and because of all the excitement, the young fan got taken away and began to enjoy himself more than he should have. After moving quickly from pub to pub, the boys settled in the 'Owain Glyndwr' to have a quiet one before the kick-off. By now, the boy with the golden ticket was slightly the worse for wear and had started to scrape his nose on the tavern walls. On noticing this, his friends, to prove they were good friends, kept feeding him more drinks, just to tip him right over the edge. By the time of kick-off, the boy had made it to the ground, after asking about 23 people for directions.

"Where's the ground...hiccup...to please, butt?" he kept asking.

Apparently, everyone thought he was taking the mick, because he was standing outside the ground gates. It was a mystery that he hadn't heard the deafening noise emanating from the ground. After being let into the ground, the boy stumbed to his seat and, rumour has it, found it hard even to sit down. By this time, he could see about 4 teams on the pitch. Trying desperately hard to focus on the players, the rugby boy thought it might be a good idea to have 'a little brandy', to sort himself out. But, strangely enough, this made things worse. By half-time, when the game was just about to get really interesting, the boy stumbled out of the stadium.

By 9.30 in the evening, his friends were starting to get worried. No one had seen or heard of him since half-time, when his mate watched him almost roll to the toilets. He was the laugh and joke of the club, up until 8.00pm, because he had missed the second-half, proabably one of the best second-halves in Welsh rugby. But, by 9.30pm, people began to get worried. Was he hurt? Had he fallen on to the railway track and been run over? Had he slipped into the Fantasy Lounge for a night-cap? All these things were going through everyone's mind, especially through the mind of the boy's mother, who was even more worried. After all, who was going to eat the sausage, beans and chips she had cooked for him?

After about three minutes of panic, everything was resolved and the panic was over. The stupid boy, who had left the stadium during the Welsh win over England, was safe and sound – in his bed. The friend had, earlier in the evening, received a drunken phone call from the 'idiot', asking what the score was. Thinking it was a joke, the friend slammed his phone down. The drunken lad, still bladdered after the the day's drinking, then took to his bed, where he remained until 10 o'clock the next morning. That is when he found out the score, and also what had happened the previous day. Needless to say, despite the throbbing head, the boy was rather gutted.

The club for whom the boy plays only allows him to buy raffle tickets for important matches if he promises one thing.

And you can guess what that is!

F – Fancy Dress

To fully appreciate fancy dress, you don't have to go on tour. The fun of dressing up and looking like a complete dick happens everywhere – usually at birthdays or on festive occasions. On tour, though, fancy dress is compulsory. For the 'normal' tourists this means dressing up for maybe one night. After all, it's quite a laugh, but for the severely deranged and outgoing tour party, fancy dress can start from when the bus leaves your rugby club and finishes when the bus returns, three to four days later. Rumour has it that this sort of thing happens quite occasionally. And the tourists that have taken part in this tomfoolery believe it should be made mandatory, if someone wishes to embark on a tour.

In some ways I agree with this sentiment. After all, it is only a bit of fun; and it would save taking a clothes bag with you.

There are many costumes that I have been totally flummoxed by over the years, including one during an international, when a rugby player came suited up in just a bin liner, with some sort of cardboard mask on his head. When asked what he came as, he croaked, "Darth Vadar," much to the delight of the home fans who were in the vicinity. The sad thing was, he really thought he looked like him. At the end of the night, though, there was a slight resemblance;

but not by the way he looked, just purely by the way he sounded.

For me, thinking back, the most infamous fancy dress costume that I can recall has, I think, been on every tour. It belongs to a good friend, and every time it is worn it is the centre of attention. Calling it a fancy dress costume might insult people who take pride in looking 'the one' when preparing for that kind of party, because it is only a beige suit, a pink shirt and a white tie. Yes, rather normal, you might say. However, don a long, permed, blond wig, colour in a moustache, and smoke a cigar, and the whole costume changes. Then, to top it off, put all this on a mad, Welsh rugby club player, and then you're in business. The suit has created so much fun that it would be hard to put every story into words. All I

"I wish someone had told me that the fancy dress was cancelled"

can say is that it has entertained thousands of people worldwide, been on TV, and brought large pubs to a standstill.

But, as with everything, good things can't last forever. Unfortunately, the suit was ripped when some boys got jealous. It was obvious they didn't believe that the person wearing it was a well-known American actor (this was obvious when the suit owner started calling everyone 'butt') and decided to rip the jacket after a fracas broke out.

That night was a sad night for everyone who knew of the suit. It now hangs in the wardrobe, with the wig, the shirt and the tie. The owner says it will never be re-sewn.

G – Glory Days and Glory Boys

Most zealous rugby fans would know exactly what I mean when I mention glory days. Most glory boys wouldn't. To me, the glory days were during the 70s, when the Welsh were virtually unbeatable. From assiduously watching tapes of the likes of Gareth Edwards, Barry John, Gerald Davies, and JPR Williams, I can see why we won so many games.

Back then, rugby in Wales was completely different: in a way, comical. I sometimes wonder how the likes of JPR ran under all that hair. And the jerseys? I'm sure that there was only one size, and whether or not you were JJ Williams or Derek Quinnell, it didn't matter – you had what you were given. Watch the videos. Either there was a mix-up with the order, or the washing machine was on the blink. But they still won! Despite looking like they'd been on the razz for three weeks (which they probably had), they still manged to win a clutch of Triple Crowns.

Don't get me wrong, I love the side of today. I'm just stating the fact that shaving your legs and gelling your hair might not guarantee you winning matches. On the other hand, having a head like a plasterer's radio might. So, that's enough about glory days. The team was near enough unbeatable back then, but it was a lot different. With the side we have today, I definitely think things are destined to happen.

Glory boys has a whole different meaning to glory days. The people who are glory boys are usually the people who have never set foot on a rugby pitch. Yes, you know who you are. These are the people who spend their weekends shopping with their missuses, moaning continuously about the lack of talent in the Welsh side. It's not a bad thing. After all, anyone can criticise the Welsh team, when they are putting their groceries on the back seat, or when they're taking a ride in the countryside, listening to Vivaldi. It's easy.

Yet these are usually the people who are down

there the next season, when Wales have won the Grand Slam. You can see them in the front row, sporting their cameras, their woolly hats, nice tattoos of a red dragon on their faces, waving their blow-up daffodils in the crowd. You can see them loving it, absorbing the atmosphere.

"C'mon, Wales. C'mon, Wales," they shout. "You're the best'."

Bear in mind, though, that a year before, Wales were the worst side in the world. "God, Wales, they couldn't score in a brothel. Ah, Wales, they're crap, mun."

Yes, they exist – and it's usually these glory boys who get caught singing the wrong words to the nationl anthem, when it is shown on the TV. But it's a bit of fun. These glory boys will always be around – especially when Wales are winning. Watch them, next time you're down the stadium. They'll probably be singing 'Delilah', when 'Bread of Heaven' comes on.

H – Hangover

'Hangovers' has to be used for my letter H, for more reasons than one. As everyone knows, hangovers are the worst things in the world. I sometimes pray to God and ask him why hangovers were invented – he hasn't got back to me. But, despite this, for all Welsh rugby players, hangovers exist. And they get worse when we go on tour.

It makes me laugh, picturing all the healthy-looking faces leaving the South Wales Valleys for a day out in Cardiff, or for the end-of-season tour. The boys are seated on the dusty coach seats, smiling, happily drinking their 6th can of lager. Their mouths shed little giggles as they look out of the window and notice the bus is only on Neath bank.

For the best drinkers, this is bliss – that place called heaven that means you can drink what you want for four days non-stop. No missus telling you what to do – just forty-five other Welsh boys doing the same. From doing my research for this book, I've heard stories of over a hundred pints being consumed on a three-day tour. One hundred pints. Can you believe it? And, apparently, that was just the bus driver.

However, not every tourist is like this. Oh, no. You can guarantee that, for every tour, there is always a tourist who will spend the holiday in bed. People reading this are probably nodding at the thought of it. On many a tour, I have seen boys get absolutely steaming on the first night, and they carry on drinking until the early hours. When they awake from their coffins, it is a different story, mind. The colour on these tourists' faces changes somewhat overnight. From looking a picture of health on the Friday, dancing and giggling, and full of vitality, the transformation is exceedingly quick. The next morning, everything can change, and the person can be seen looking extremely yellow – like someone out of The Simpsons. The victim will lie in bed for days, in complete darkness, slowly wasting away, one hand under a pillow, the other resting in a sick bowl. It is not a pleasant sight to see, looking at your friend and thinking of a chicken korma. But it is a part of tour. Having good mates to check on you every day is good enough for any tourist. A quick grunt ensures that the tourist is okay, and the rest of the Welsh rugby club boys can carry on drinking.

This can go on for days, usually until the tour comes to an end. 'What a waste of a tour,' you might be saying. In some ways, I agree and ask myself the same thing. But people still end up going, basically because they're afraid they might miss something.

To hit the nail on the head, they'd prefer to stay in their hotel beds, looking like Homer Simpson than be at home. After all, it is tour time!

I – Idiots

Where you stay while you're on tour is quite important. Digs – or accommodation for the posh people – have been discussed already in this book, but they need to be analysed a little deeper. That's why I have chosen Idiots for my letter I. Being rugby boys, sometimes people assume that we are dull.

"Ai, they must be dull to play rugby, mun, getting their heads smashed in every week."

And these accusations are sometimes right, because sometimes rugby players can act dull, or, better still, be total idiots.

When staying in a hotel on tour, the manager usually asks some questions. You know, the typical questions that hotel managers usually ask when they have 45 Welsh tourists staying at the hotel:

"What is your name?"
"Where are you from?"
"Are you going to ruin my hotel?"

And these questions are answered with veracity. After all, the boys are soberish when they arrive and have no plans about throwing the TV out of the window. So, everything is fine for the first few hours. The manager appears to like the Welsh rugby boys and is probably wondering why people tar them all with the same brush. After all, if the rugby boys do get drunk, why would they want to do anything to the hotel? They have, at the end of the day, left a deposit of £500 to pay for anything that should get broken.

Two and a half days later, things change somewhat, some of the tourists become a little rowdier and some even turn into 'idiots'. This is the time when things change drastically and you realise that the £500 deposit left in the 'nice' manager's reception area might never ever be seen again.

The typical things happen – they have probably happened on most tours. The party of tourists goes out and has a good drink. A few of the party decide to go home early because they're rather drunk, and the rest of the boys stay out and think nothing of it.

When everyone returns to the hotel, a couple of

"Jesus, John, how much did Dai drink last night?!"

hours later, they find the boys, who had left four hours earlier, sitting outside the hotel with their bags. Slightly confused, on entering the hotel, you see the manager looking rather vexed and holding a fire extinguisher. Then, when you go into the boys' room and notice the TV broken, and the bed turned upside down, you realise that there hasn't been a fire, but that the idiots have gone crazy in their rooms. It is by this time that you know that the £500 deposit will never be seen again. In fact, you can almost picture the manager buying a new set of golf clubs out of it.

But, after all, it is a laugh. Especially when you hear the explanation for the broken TV.

"I dunno why it's broken. I only had a piss in it!"

That's capital I for Idiot.

J – Joking Around

Being born in Wales, it is a requirement to like jokes, and it a requirement to have a joke around.

For me, the banter in rugby is something that you never experience anywhere else. This is purely because of the zany characters that Welsh rugby boasts. Most of this joking around, as these stories suggest, involves a lot of stupidity; and this humour, sometimes, is not everyone's cup of tea. For instance, my local rugby club prides itself on the Obvious Game. Many of you might not have heard of this notorious Valley pastime, but it is a crowd pleaser in this little club. To play it, you must have someone who can tell a good joke and simply keep a straight face. All it involves is picking on someone who doesn't know about it, and someone who simply believes the game to be damn well childish. Or, you can just pick on a fellow rugby player, who knows the game inside out, but who, unfortunately, is rather dim.

Some good examples of this entertainment are as follows:

A good one to play – which is still played on unsuspecting customers – usually involves a tired barmaid, who is coming toward the end of a shift, and some adolescent, tipsy rugby players. Picture the scene. It is nearing half-past eleven and the petite, pretty barmaid has been serving the youngsters all night. The music has stopped and the lights are coming on. Like an idiot, the one boy asks: "Do you work here?" to which the reply is: "Course I do. What? You think I'm behind here for nothing," as she smiles and tells the other members of staff about the ludicrous question.

But little does she know that she has just been a victim of the Obvious Game, which she will realise later, when she is asked a further ten times, much to the delight of the tipsy rugby boys.

Another classic involves a dim rugby player. After chatting to him for about half an hour about a man who played for South Wales Police, I asked him what the player in question did for a living. Simply not thinking that he was going to be a victim, the dim rugby player answered confidently, "He works for the police, don't he?" But it was too late. He had already said it.

Other stories have simply involved the ridiculously obvious jokes, like walking past a police station and asking someone where the local police station is, or asking someone where you can post a letter, while you are standing outside a post office. These people are the best to ask because you can gaurantee that they will do the stupid thing and point. They simply think you're incredibly thick, and you laugh to yourself, knowing that they have just been competitors in the Really Ridiculous Obvious Game.

These stories might go right over people's heads, and some people might think they are unbelievably childish. And I agree, because they are bloody childish. But, on the other hand, they do raise some laughs.

Apart from these really stupid games, some other silly games have been involved in Welsh rugby. These are just some of them:

The phone call trick is a classic. It is usually used when a rugby club is full to the rafters. All it needs is for somoene to pick up the phone and start talking. Eveyone involved knows the crack, except for the player who will fall for the prank. It goes something like this:

"Dai, phone call for you, butt."

"Who is it?"

"Dunno, think it's your missus."

"Oh, what does she want now? I said I'd be home by half-seven. What time is it now?"

"Quarter-past nine." *Boy grabs phone and starts to speak very loudly:* "Hello. Hello." *To boys:* "Can't hear anything, boys. All I can hear are pips. Hello, hello. Jan, is that you? I can't hear anything, love. I'll be home soon, I promise. Tara." *To barmaids:* "You wanna sort that phone out, mun; you can't hear no one speaking on the other end."

Then, as he walks back to his seat, he is none the wiser as his friends laugh to themselves in the corner. As with most jokes, the victim normally knows he's had the mick taken out of him, after picking up the phone for the seventh time. This is when he realises that he's been shouting into the phone, when there is no one on the other end, and looking like a complete idiot, while the whole club was watching.

Jokes with the phone can differ immensely. Having someone pretend they're someone else can be a corker if executed right. I've seen people leave watching the internationals down the club earlier than usual because they've had phone calls saying their Chinese is ready. It's only when they get to the Chinese take-away that they realise they didn't make the order.

Jokes like this are a massive part of the social side of rugby in Wales. It's great fun to see people having a laugh with each other and still playing pranks. So, to end on the letter 'J' with this joke would be quite fitting.

Once upon a time, there was this bloke called Wilson and everybody knew him. Some days, he'd be working on his machine in the factory, when famous people would walk in and start talking to him. One day, Prince Charles walked in and, before doing anything, went straight over to Wilson to have a good old chin-wag. After Charlie had left, the others were in total disbelief and wondered how on earth Prince Charles knew sad, old Wilson.

"I'm telling you, boys, everyone knows me. Me and Charlie go back years."

Totally taken aback, Wilson's work mates kept on badgering Wilson.

"Everyone knows you? What a load of crap, mun. I suppose even the Pope knows you," one of them said.

"To be honest, me and Pope are also very close.

Of course he'd know me," replied Wilson.

Overhearing this, the boss was laughing in the corner of the factory at Wilson.

"You know the Pope?" he said.

"Yeah," Wilson replied.

"Well, I"ve got a bet for you. If you think you know the Pope, I will fly you out to the Vatican so you can meet him. Up for it?" asked the boss.

"Well course I am. Haven't seen him for ages. Be nice to catch up. And I'll get a free holiday!" replied Wilson.

Two weeks later, the boss, Wilson and a few of his workmates are outside the Vatican. The boss thought it was money well spent, to see Wilson ridiculed in front of his mates. As the group stood outside the Vatican, Wilson's boss pointed to the Pope, who was standing on the balcony outside waving.

"Right, to win this bet, Wilson, you have to get up with the Pope and wave to everyone of us down here," the boss said, pointing to the few thousand onlookers.

"Easy," replied Wilson. "I'll be about half an hour."

As Wilson made his way off, his boss and workmates waited for Wilson to make a fool out of himself. However, half an hour later, the boss couldn't believe his eyes as Wilson stood on the balcony with his arms around the Pope's shoulders.

He couldn't believe what he was seeing. Another hour passed, and down came Wilson, to see his boss and workmates all lying on the floor. They had all fainted. Worrying slightly, Wilson got down on his hands and knees and started tapping his boss across his face. Finally, his boss woke up.

"I can't believe it," said Wilson's boss. "It's incredible"

"I suppose you fainted when you saw me up there with the Pope," said Wilson.

"No," replied the bemused boss, "I fainted when this French fella tapped me on the back and asked, "Who's that up there with Wilson?"

K – Karaoke

For any Welsh rugby fan, singing is something that we all love. Most of us sing anywhere: in the bath, in the shower, in the car, in work – the list goes on. We Welsh love it. I am not sure why this is. Maybe it's because we have great singers in Wales, like Tom Jones, Kelly Jones from the Stereophonics, James Dean Bradfield from the Manic Street Preachers, and so on. And then there's the local bands, like 4th Street Traffic, who, I'm sure, will get a good record deal one day.

But, forget all these. What about the real singers,

who get up on karaoke when they go away? Isn't this part of the rugby culture in Wales? Within Welsh rugby there is singing wherever you go. The coach journey is the place where it starts, as the tourists get ready for their annual four-day booze-up. Songs like 'Delilah', 'Roll a Silver Dollar', and 'Bread of Heaven' can be heard echoing from the coach windows. The boys love it. They think they're the greatest singers and cannot believe that none of them has got a record deal.

Then, when the night is upon them, and a few more beers have been consumed, there is always one of the tour party that wants to sing on karaoke. For most of us, singing is a bit of laugh – the thing you do to create an atmosphere. It raises spirits, relieves tired muscles and soothes aching heads. It is a dulcet and refreshing balm for us Welsh.

However, even though we think this, singing shouldn't be taken too seriously, especially if the person who thinks he can sing can't. One tourist decided to try and emulate Robbie Williams, and sang 'Angels' in this pub. Despite having a few drinks, the boy could speak quite clearly, and he appeared quite confident as he took the stage. Bear in mind, though, the singers before him were of the highest quality, and there was some good money for the eventual winner.

With his bald head, and his beer belly sticking out of his jeans, the wannabe singer bore no resemblance to Robbie Williams. Robbie Coltrane with a skinhead, yes, but not Robbie Williams. And when he sang, you could have said the same. Embarrassing is not the correct word to describe the singing. Well, if you could call it that. Everyone stared in amazement at the Welsh lad as he attempted to belt out the song. The worst thing about it was that he was actually getting into it, even pulling all the facial expressions that singers pull while singing. You could see by his face that he was thoroughly enjoying his time up on stage. The harsh reality, though, was the fact that it sounded like the local cat sanctuary being burnt to the ground.

After coming from the stage, a clap could be heard coming from the bar. The singer smiled proudly as he heard this. It was only later that we found out that the 'clapper' was in fact deaf and dumb and couldn't hear any of the screeching.

So, tourists, beware of the phantom singers. If anyone thinks they can sing, ask them to do a rehearsal first, just to see if they fit the bill. If they don't, just hide the microphone from them; or just stay out of the karaoke bars.

L – Liars

Yes, you've got it – it's lying. Or, if you're Welsh and five years of age, fibbing. For most of these tell-tale people, they probably do not even realise that not lying is one of the Ten Commandments. But it doesn't bother that particular Welsh rugby boy, when he's having a drink. Oh, no! Being a liar comes naturally to some people. There is a guy from my local rugby club who loves to tell the odd porkie. A lovely man he may well be, but he does lie quite a bit. During his time coaching our youth and first team side, we were told that every one of the back-row forwards who we were going to play against had had a Welsh cap. During that time in the youth, we were convinced that every back-row opposition was going to be awesome. We soon realised that it was almost impossible to have five thousand Ex-Welsh backrow players come up against us.

Lies, however, do not just exist in my little club. Lies are ubiquitous in Wales and have been around in Welsh rugby for decades. Some of these lies can be harmless – a little bit of banter with your fellow players and fans. To really get a taste of lying in Welsh rugby, I think we have to look at the kind of lies that we hear about in Welsh rugby:

The Blatantly Obvious Lie has been used in every rugby village in Wales, and can differ in each one. A popular one can involve an under 16s rugby match, where there is always one player who looks far too old to still be playing in the side. The boy (well, man!) in question can usually be seen trying to hide behind the rest of the team, but his six-foot three frame and bristly moustache cannnot evade the ref's glance. Then, the conversation goes something like this:

"Honest, ref. I'm 17. Ask my mother."

"Don"t lie to me, son. I saw you pull up in the car park in your E-Reg Ford. Can you please leave the field?"

So that's the blatantly obvious lie.

The Drunken Lie happens after the match, usually towards the end of the evening. The Welsh rugby fan, barely able to stand up, can be seen trying to enter a night-club. Obviously seriously drunk, the bouncer stops him and tells hims he's had too much. After a slight disagreement lasting for about five minutes, the bouncer can be heard asking:

"How many you had?"

To which the reply is:

"Only three, honest. I've got the car with me."

The drunken lie – it happens everywhere.

The Cheating Lie is a classic lie for dodgy linesmen. These lies are so dodgy that even friends of the man with the flag cannot bear to watch. This sort of deceit is great for the home team but quite a heinous crime for the away team. More often than not, this kind of lie happens at the finale of a match, when the scores are even. Both sides are desperate to win, and so is the linesman. Normally, a kick is awarded on the touchline, which just shaves the inside of the post. Everyone can see it, apart from the linesman, who puts his flag up. The home team is jubilant, the away team severely livid at the cheating, lying linesman, as they walk off the pitch as losers. During times like this, it's great to watch the linesman trying to dig himself out of his hole.

"It was the wind. Honest, it trickled over. I'd never lie. Oh, it was 13 : 10, was it. Close game!"

The Cruel Lie can be quite harsh to the players on the receiving end. These lies normally take place on the Thursday before a game, when a particular side hasn't got a game. After being put into the pool, the club usually receives a phone call inviting them to play against a side from another valley.

"Yeah, it'll be our seconds. Our firsts are away this week," the fixture secretary from the other club will say.

And eveyone's happy, as it should be a fair match between two second team sides. That's until they get on the pitch, to find out that they have been a victim of the cruel lie, because in front of them are very mean, tall and strong-looking men, who are obviously the club's first team.

After getting stuffed 107-0, you can see the

nefarious grin on the fixture secretary's face
as he gloats over his team's win, much to the
embarrassment and anger of the bruise-ridden away
team.

The Childish Lie is a lie that is normally played
on the stupidest member of the rugby team, and it is
normally the heartless joker who plays it. I have only
ever known this to happen once, and I admit I did
laugh. Despite this, I did feel some kind of sympathy
for the player involved.

The lie has probably been done many times in
Welsh rugby, because that's the type of people we are.
The whole joke was acted out quite well. The player
who was getting tucked up had not been training
that week but still wanted to play on the Saturday.
Phoning the club on the Saturday, he politely asked
where the second team game was being played.
Amidst an echo of giggles, the player was told that
the seconds were away, to a side in another valley,
quite far away. He was also told that the kick-off
was earlier than usual, and to have his kit on when
he got to the pitch. The player swallowed all this,
little knowing that his team were playing home. It
wasn't until four hours later, when he walked into a
clubhouse of howling players, that he realised he had
been the victim of a very childish joke!

The Ridiculous Lie will be the last lie that
I mention. It involves our national side, Wales,

and its coaching set-up. It might be me, but does everyone agree that the 2006 Six Nations campaign was an incredibly farcical time for the WRU? It all happened too quickly for it to have some credibility, and, in a lot of ways, you could see why many avid Welsh fans thought the stories that emanated from the WRU panel were somewhat spurious.

I love Wales and its national team, but the news that came out in February made me think and question the whole saga. The funny thing is, all the people involved in camp said they didn't know anything about it and that everything was fine with Mike Ruddock. Gareth Thomas is one of my heroes in the Welsh side, but witnessing him being pilloried on *Scrum V* was quite embarassing. He was obviously covering up something. However, it's a lie that will breathe for many years in Welsh rugby. Let's just hope that, because we love the Welsh side that much, lies are eradicated and that we can start winning Grand Slams again.

M – Madness

Madness is a word you do not hear very often. Or, if you do, you usually associate it with axe murderers and people like that. In this book, *The A-Z of Welsh Rugby*, I have chosen Madness for my letter M. The reason for my decision is obvious, because many people think that to play the game of rugby, one has to be mad. My missus thinks this. Even though she loves to watch from the side, dressed in her fur coat, hat and scarf, and high-heeled boots, she sometimes wonders why I ever took up the game. It was only after she said so that I started to think about my life in rugby.

It suddenly struck me how rough the game is. It is utter madness. The name of the game in rugby is to score on your opponents' line. Yes, great. Throughout youth, the game was rough, but as I worked my way into the firsts, I was to realise how rough rugby would become.

By this time, our side was playing sides from all across the Rhondda. This is when I first thought about this crazy game, and started to think about the rules of rugby. "Must score over opponents' line," I would say to myself. But it wasn't as easy as that. When you have the ball and you're running up the line, no one ever explained to me that these Rhondda boys would want to kill me first, rather than let me put the ball over their line. So, today, thinking about the missus saying I must be mad to play rugby, she might be right, because the game is mad.

Another thing in rugby you can associate with madness ties in sweetly with rugby tours and drinking. This is when you see the other side of madness. From talking to people about their tour tales, I sometimes wonder if you can associate drinking with madness. And, just to clarify my suspicions, I read some health books, and, funnily enough, they do go hand in hand. But, just to ease people's concerns, this is very rare. Apparently it would take a lot of drinking to lead to madness.

"I can assure you, Carwyn, you're not a motocycle!"

However, I do believe that some people go a bit loopy while on tour. It's strange to see people doing things they don't normally do. It's strange to see people who have never said a dicky bird all year down the rugby club, suddenly climbing up on the pub roof in a Superman outfit. It's strange to see the father of a first team player eating blue chalk, and telling the chairman that he hadn't seen it when the chairman asked where the chalk was. And it was even stranger to watch the chairman asking the father why he had a blue mouth.

Stranger than this was witnessing the captain of the first team side pretending he was a motorbike. There was very busy traffic at the time and people were wondering what the hold-up was. Straining their eyes to see, the annoyed drivers behind could just about make out a boy on his knees, with another boy on top of him, acting as rider, making motorbike noises. "Why?" you ask. "That's a bit childish." Yes, you're right. But you don't think about that, after having no sleep and you've been drinking for three days.

For this story, four Welsh boys, who were touring down in West Wales at that time, happened to love the sea, especially when they've had a drink. Away from the rest of the 'normal' tourist party, the boys decided to go it alone and drink in the seaside bars. After copious amounts of alcohol had been consumed, the conversation turned to the sea, and, after roughly five minutes, a bet was made. It was rather a silly bet, when you look at how drunk they were. It was a challenge to see how far they could swim out to sea with no clothes on. Being typical Welsh rugby boys, all four agreed.

After stopping at an off-licence to buy some drink to take with them, the boys set off over the sand dunes, and headed towards the part of the sea where you were allowed to swim. You know the area: not far from the rocks, by the place with the really strong current. Because all were good swimmers, not one of the boys really worried about drowning. After all, what harm can twelve pints of lager do you, if you want a nice swim? However, take the lager into consideration, and the finished bottle of vodka, and you know that 'the swim' might not be as straightforward as it seems.

Three hours later, and half a mile out at sea, a man reported seeing four human heads bobbing up and down. This was a cause of great concern for the caravan owner, who couldn't believe his eyes when he saw this. The lifeguards also shared the same feelings as they picked up the four drunken Welsh boys from the sea. However, with everyone in a panic, the boys, still half-cut from the day's boozing, were wondering why the race had been stopped, and who was going to win the bet. Needless to say, the lifeguards weren't happy.

But that's drunken Welsh boys for you. They sometimes simply don't think, do they?

N – Naked

For those fortunate enough to have gone on a tour, I am sure that most will be well acquainted with the word 'naked'. I believe myself to be telling the truth when I say that, with every tour that I've been on, someone out of the tour party has found himself scantily clad.

On hearing these 'naked' stories, one might assume that it is often a member of the younger generation who finds himself unclothed. However, to make this assumption would be a misapprehension. On one particular tour, one of the player's fathers, Dombie, decided that, whilst singing one of his favourite songs ('Myfanwy', I believe it was), he would sing it with his trousers around his ankles. He said it gave the song more 'emphasis', when someone asked him about the incident later.

It was also funny to witness the old man's son talking to one of the locals. When the local villager asked the teenager who this strange, naked man was, without a tint of embarrassment, the boy answered quite proudly, "Oh, that's my father." Priceless.

Later that evening, you could hear the shouts of,

"Like father, like son," echoing through the streets as the young son ran totally naked along the busy streets of Exmouth.

One of the most memorable 'naked' moments has to be the time when Wales beat Ireland to win the Grand Slam in 2005. This was quite an unexpected moment for the party of tourists, because the player in question had been alone for most of the match. It was rumoured that the management wanted the boy to be left on his own purely because he was, excuse the cliché, 'drunk as a skunk'.

In the lounge of the local rugby club that the tour party was drinking in, the final whistle finally went. The Welsh boys went mental – tables were kicked over and glasses were smashed. One English boy was well pissed off about this because a new pair of glasses was to cost him £150 at his local opticians. The Welsh boys could not believe it. Even the English boys from Bournemouth couldn't believe it. Not only had Wales won the Grand Slam, but some Welsh boys had taken over their clubhouse. As the chants of "Wales, Wales" boomed through the club, out of the midst of broken glass and red shirts came a drunken, naked Welsh boy. His rugby team mates looked on in disbelief as he trampled over the tables, his meat and two veg dangling in the air. The local English boys (and women!) couldn't believe what they were seeing. This total disbelief would continue, as they watched from the clubhouse window while seven of the other players, too, took off their clothes.

After doing a couple of laps of honour in the warm May sun, the boys returned to face a vexed rugby chairman, with a dustpan and brush in one hand, and seven pairs of pants in the other. It was a time that will not be forgotten.

O – On the Pull

Some wives and girlfriends have this silly suspicion that a tour is a time for meeting new women. From my take on this, I would say this is wrong, because, from my experience, being able to speak to a girl would be a start, let alone doing anything else. But for some youngsters who are single, going away is a time to learn a few things: it's a time to learn how to drink three pints in 10 seconds; a time to stay awake after being out for almost 27 hours; and it's also a time to meet new girls. For many rookie tourists this will be the highlight of the trip – especially if that boy is not attached; and he will see a different life to what he's normally used to, drinking in the valleys.

First of all, when chatting to a girl while on tour – and this is more important if you are away in England – you need to be coherent in your speech. One thing a typical English girl hates is a conversation that is devoid of clarity. So, the first rule is to avoid getting to the 20 pint mark if you want even a chance of a girl saying "hello" to you.

Another important thing I've noticed about young, naive, single Welsh boys is the fact that they don't care who they try to chat up. A girl can be with a group of boys – all over 6 ft tall – and he wouldn't give a damn. I've sometimes asked myself if some of these kamikaze boys have tunnel vision, when they walk towards the young filly in question. Obviously not, when you see the youngster being propelled through the air. So, that's rule number two: have a look who the girl's with before asking her, "Do you come here often?"

When these predators, having been drinking all day, find themselves hitting the dance floor, they think they're like John Travolta as they slide across the floor. The reality is completely different, and this is evident from the looks on the girls' faces, when they see this drunken idiot doing the Okey Cokey without even knowing it. The boy in question then decides to try again to grab the same girl who's just spurned his advances, the end result being a smack in the mouth. So, rule number 3 is: just don't dance after an all-dayer, and keep your hands to yourself.

The next rule involves a laugh, especially if you're having a session with the boys. However, sometimes this rule needs to be avoided, if the girls involved do not like a joke. The tomfoolery originally started on a tour to Liverpool and had all the boys in stitches. It's quite a good pulling technique for all budding Adonises, but it has to be executed well. All you do is stand at the corner of the dance floor, acting cool, while you drink your pint. At this moment, you are the eagle and the girl is your prey. When the prey has been detected (in other words, you have made eye contact), call her over by a continual wave of your hand. This is the time when all the other drinkers are watching in anticipation. Then, when the girl slowly sidles over, her hair swaying from side to side, you smile at her.

"Alright," she will say hopefully, as she smiles back.

And then you hit her with it:

"Yes, great, love – bloody hot in here, though, innit?"

Classic. By this time, all the boys are in stitches and the girl is left humiliated. But this is the moment of truth. If the girl smiles, then you're on a winner. But, if she doesn't, be prepared to have a smack in the jaw. So, rule number 4, try to avoid taking the mick out of a girl. Or, if you do try it, try to make sure that it's done with effect. That way, you avoid a sore cheek and you might get more that a doner kebab on the way home.

These small rules show some sympathy towards

these youngsters, purely because, after 20 pints, they simply forget what they're doing. No disrespect to anyone here, but when a roookie Welsh tourist is drunk, he'll try and pull anyone. That includes girls, nans, boys, sheep – the list goes on.

I watched one of these boys in action as he kissed over 10 women. To this day, I swear there wasn't a set of teeth amongst any of them. So, for any budding tourist who's single, take these tips into consideration before going on the pull. You could find yourselves in a 'sticky' position.

P – Police Station

It wasn't hard to think of something for P. It's not that I am a hardened criminal – in fact, I've never been arrested – it's just that most outings involving Welsh rugby clubs might involve some run-ins with the police. Some incidents might be serious, though there are very few of these. Some incidents, on the other hand, are more light-hearted, and it is nice to know that the drunken Welsh and the English police can get along.

Most policemen and policewomen I know are sound as a pound. Just to prove this, my own sister, Joanne, is a copper, and I think she is doing pretty well. Trouble is, I haven't spoken to her since she joined the force. Nah, but seriously, if you treat the police with respect, then you will, 99 percent of the time, get respect back. This is evident on tour, from my experiences. It might be me, but the police seem to like the Welsh Valleys' sort of humour, when we are on tour. They like to have a joke with us and have a laugh, even though they cannot understand what we are saying. However, they do get a bit annoyed when we pinch their hats, so try to avoid this.

The story I am going to enlighten you with happened many years ago. It involved a gang of drunken rugby players from a town not far from Cardiff. Again, lots of drink was consumed, as this was a rugby team. And it was the late 1970s, which meant that drinking didn't really matter, if you were a rugby player. Not like these days, when you can get fined for having a shandy on a Tuesday before a match.

The party of players left the pub just before stop-tap, whatever time it was in those days. Not wanting to go home, the sozzled lads decided to call in on the local Indian for a sit-down meal. Twelve vindaloos later, washed down by another four pints of strong bitter each, the boys were arguing about the bill.

"Let's do a runner," the one said.

"Ai, come on, then," the others chirupped.

Fifteen minutes later, and the boys were being chased by the Indians and the local policemen. Little did the boys know that they were being closed in; this was mainly due to young Dai, who had broken his leg in a game against a local side the week before.

"Can't you hop faster, Dai?" the boys asked.

But it was no use. The only thing they could do was hide. They all went in different directions. Within five minutes, all but two were caught, and it wasn't long before they were all within the police's

"So do you come here often then love?"

grasp. One of the boys was caught having a piss against a house wall, and Dai, with the broken leg, got caught behind the bushes. Coppers reckoned they could see his crutch poking out. But, despite all the chasing, all the boys got was a ticking off; and they had to pay the Indian in full. So, next time, when you do a runner from the police, just make sure that none of your party has a broken leg!

Q – Quarrels, arguments and fights

No, I'm not talking about life at home with the missus, I'm talking about Welsh rugby and all the aggro that goes with it. But, you see, that's just the point. People would think that, because most rugby players are quite big, strong and muscular, we're all natural fighters. However, not all rugby players are like this. Take me, for example. I'm far from muscular, and I'd rather stick pins in my eyes than have a toe-to-toe with someone.

People's perceptions of rugby players are slightly harsh and totally wrong. I still hear girls mumbling to their friends:

"Oh, don't bother with him, he's a rugby boy."

Even my wife used to say it to me. So, what is wrong with us Welsh rugby boys? Yeah, fair enough, we do like a drink, and we like to take our clothes off when we've had a few sherbets. But does this matter? We still get up for work and to live our normal lives. Rugby doesn't make us different, or turn us into monsters. And this is where it all gets a bit hazy. As I've said, because rugby is a physical game, and a lot of the players are physical, the people assume that we are thugs. OK, so the game of rugby does bring out a lot of aggression, and there are times when players do tend to start hitting other players, especially when testicles have been grabbed and eyes gouged. To be fair, though, this is part of the game, and many fans like to witness a good old scrap. As soon as you hear the old '99' call, you can see the fans' faces glued to the pitch as they witness an almighty scrap.

But, despite many players looking like John Merrick, in the clubhouse the fighting has stopped and everyone is friends again. It is even surreal to watch two very hard and ugly men talk over a pint, when, only half an hour earlier, they were trying to kill one another. It's great to hear the conversation. It goes something like this:

"Cracking game?"

"Ai."

"What was the score?"

"Dunno."

"Good fighting, though."

"Great, part of the game, innit? Think I broke my

nose again."

"Yeah, I hit you from the side."

"Don't worry 'bout it, it'll mend. Are these your teeth?"

"Oh, cheers, butt. What're you drinking?"

"Mine's a pint of rough, please. Cheers, son."

Crazy, isn't it? They've just hit ten lumps of shit out of one another and now they're having a pint. But this is the point I am making. Despite scrapping on the rugby pitch, these players can still have a drink and a chat after the game. They can put their problems behind them. That's what frustrates me when people call rugby players thugs. Unlike football fans, whose sport is not that physical, the fighting stops as soon as they walk off the pitch. No disrespect to football lovers, but, personally, I can't understand why there is so much violence in football. It completely baffles me – because it's such a glamorous sport.

So, to end this old fable of rugby players being called thugs, I can tell you that it's a load of old codswallop. The only quarreling rugby players and fans do after a game is with their loved ones, as they waltz into the house at half-past 12, when they should have been at home at 7. Now that's an argument!

R – Referee

There any many stories that are associated with the letter R – rugby being the obvious one. However, because this book is about Welsh rugby and the fun that goes with it, I have elected to write about referees. All you rugby enthusiasts probably know many humorous stories regarding the man in the middle, especially if your team plays in the lower divisions. Top athletes – those who play above Division 1 in the Heineken League – are not used to having bad referees. For instance, you can put your hands in a ruck knowing that your fingers will not be broken, purely because good refs will spot that kind of thing. But playing in the lower leagues, rugby is a totally different ball game.

I symphasise a lot with referees, because they do get a lot of stick. If you are a player, getting a bit of aggro off the opposite side can be a bit of fun; and this is mainly because there are fifteen of you in a side. However, being a ref is totally disparate. I've played in games and cringed, having heard some of the abuse the refs get.

In one particular game, the ref had had continual abuse all game. In my eyes, he wasn't doing a bad job: it's just a pity that he had forgotten his whistle. After the match, I can remember some drunken supporters asking the ref why he hadn't opened his eyes when the opposition threw a forward pass. Looking somewhat sad, I watched the ref dash off to the changing room; he was obviously upset. It was only when I saw him in his dressing room that I noticed his false eye. There was further banter when he came in the showers with us – the home team. To this day, the boys still talk about the camp ref, who stared at everyone's family allowance. Obviously, they didn't know, and so I just kept my mouth shut and went along with it!

Having done research for this book, the funniest refereeing story I've heard epitomises the Welsh sort of humour. After hearing this story, I must admit I showed no sympathy. I say this because, after hearing the tale from a number of good sources, including the vicar of that particular village, that referee deserved to be punished. I don't mean beaten, I just mean that he deserved to have 'a bit back'. The ref during this game was utterly one-sided and gave everything to his own team. Apparently, he used to play for the club, and many people supporting the home team even said that it was the most biased refereeing that they had ever seen.

One of the players, who was on the other side that day, was so vexed by the inept refereeing that he decided to play a little joke on him. As a result, after having a shower, the player in question sneaked into the dressing room of the victim and proceeded to pinch his socks and shoes. Needless to say, after the footwear was tossed into the local river, the after-match speeches were interrupted by roars of laughter as players and supporters, from both sides, watched the ref eat his sausage and chips in bare feet.

Apparently, he hasn't reffed a game since. It's not that he doesn't want to; he's just too tight to buy a new pair of boots.

S – Star Wars Bar

Most people reading this book have probably seen the Star Wars films. They're great fun – full of energy, excitement and littered with special effects. As a kid, I must have watched the original three films at least a hundred times; I simply couldn't get enough of Princess Leia.

Now that I am older, I am still a big fan of these amazing films, so much so that the original film – Star Wars – has had a mention in my book. Readers of this book may be slightly befuddled by this, and wondering how on earth Welsh rugby can be associated with Star Wars. Well, it's quite simple really. First, just to clear up some mystery: Harrison Ford has not got a Welsh grandfather, and no, Chewbacca did not jump in the line-out for Wales – though I do admit there is some resemblance to past second-rows.

The reason why Star Wars has a mention is this. In welsh rugby, there are pubs and clubs we visit that are somewhat – how can I put it? – rough around the edges: in other words – a shit hole. And in these unkempt pubs and clubs there are usually very bizarre and weird and wonderful characters, some of whom have a striking likeness to the creatures in Star Wars.

These characters, despite not looking the most welcoming, are, in fact, friendly people. However, years of drinking in the same old pub or rugby club have taken their toll on many of these characters. They love Saturdays, purely because this is the highlight of their week, when they can watch their beloved rugby sides play; plus, it's an excuse to get blotto and act like one of the creatures out of Star Wars. However, it's not just the people who look slightly dishevelled. Many of the clubs they drink in are not the most picturesque. Having played rugby for a number of years, sometimes the places you drink in after the match do look like the bar in the first Star Wars film.

From outside, some of these clubs look like prisons; some even have bars on the inside. Also, signs littered with spelling mistakes can be seen outside the clubs:

THE USE OF MOTORBIKES ARE

PROHIBITAD HEAR; 'NO MOTERBIKES AROUND ERE' – and these signs are written by the council! Sometimes, the guarantee is that there will either be a shopping trolley outside, or a pram. These predictions are nearly always right, because normally, sitting not far from the clubhouse, slowly rusting away, are old shopping trolleys. Fantastic.

Walking into a place like this is also something to remember. First thing you notice is that the local window cleaner must have a sander, because nearly every window is boarded up. By this time, people are sometimes slightly hesitant about entering. After all, it is the unknown- and who wants to be thrown into Jabba the Hutt's pit?

Inside, for the first half an hour or so, the visitors are faced with a scene with which they are not well acquainted. As it's a Saturday – rugby day – the clubs are busier than usual. Customers stand by the bar, drinking and smoking underneath a sign that says: 'No standing, drinking or smoking at the bar'. Women, with tattoos on their arms, are arm wrestling in the corner of the room, and drunken youths can be seen sleeping on pool tables. The scene is wild.

At first, there is a nervous feeling bubbling inside your body – a feeling that you just don't want to speak to anyone, in case you might offend him or her. In some strange twist of nature, however, after a few pints and a chat with the locals about the game,

"Look, I don't care what you say, it was a fair tackle."

you realise that, even though they might look like extras from Star Wars, they are in fact good people and are unlikely to eat you.

People reading this are probably nodding, as they think back to all the rough pubs and clubs they have been in after rugby matches. It doesn't hurt though, does it, because there's always a warm reception in the clubhouse? Possibly the best clubs I've been to have been a bit shabby and tough. But, then again, that's part of Welsh rugby; the fact that you have to play these teams can be daunting, but can also be a total scream. This is purely down to the characters that drink in these pubs and clubs.

So, next time you're a bit cautions about a pub, don't worry about it; just go in and have a drink. You'll have a great time after the rugby. And who knows, you might get Chewbacca's autograph!

T – The Half-time Whistle

This whistle is always blown at half-time. This is the time that tickles me, and most certainly needs a mention in this book. The whistle indicates a rest – and from my playing days in rugby, this could mean quite a bit.

To some, the half-time whistle during a match means you have time for a fag or maybe two. It seems strangely ironic, watching these players going to the side of the pitch to their mates, to pinch a fag, whilst saying: "Jesus, I can hardly breathe." Yet still it happens.

To some, half-time means you can have a can of lager – just to make you feel refreshed. These players can then be seen keeling over, about twenty minutes into the second half, muttering: "Shit, I shouldn't have had that can."

But amazingly, and this still makes me laugh, the half-time whistle means you can nip off to the changing room toilets to, excuse the colloquial use of diction, drop the kids off. This, you might think, is not that bad. However, when you let the referee wait twenty minutes to start the second half, you could say it is slightly taking the piss. I sometimes wonder if that little jaunt to the toilets did slightly persuade the ref to give that iffy penalty.

When I think about the half-time whistle, though, my mind always trickles back to the Millennium Stadium. It might be me, but this is the worst time during the whole day. When the whistle goes, you can see everyone automatically get up, each person either thinking about going to the toilet or getting a drink. And, usually, I am right.

As you walk up the steps to the toilets and refreshment area, forty-two thousand go with you.

"What do you reckon we should do?" your best friend asks. "The queue for a pint is three miles long, but I think the one for the pisser is about four and a half."

And by the time you've decided, the whistle has blown for the second half. Then, it's time to waddle on back down the stairs, bladder still full, with a mouth like Ghandi's flip-flop, trying desperately not to bump into anyone as you clamber back to your seat.

Yeah. The half-time whistle. It's a funny, but annoying, old thing.

U – Unusual Activities

The social side of rugby is the main reason why this book has been written. It is to let strangers to rugby know the shenanigans and tomfoolery that exist after a game. So, for the letter U, I have decided to write about unusual activities. These activities, through the eyes of a rugby player or fan, might not appear unusual; however, to an outsider they would. Usually, the laughter and monkey business involved are linked with the social side of rugby, not necessarily when matches are being played. For example, having someone neck a pint of Strongbow in less than four seconds as he prepares to put a ball into the scrum just wouldn't be appropriate during a game. Plus, I am sure the ref would have something to say. On the other hand, doing this afterwards is part of the game – a prerequisite for all ardent rugby people.

Spending time in the clubhouse is probably the main reason why people go to rugby matches. This doesn't take anything away from the rugby team itself, because, obviously, the social games and singing would be non-existent if it were not for the actual playing. However, after the games – and this is evident from playing for my local side, Penallta – this is the time when fans and players can unite and, as a result, entertain not only themselves, but other people.

These are just some of the unusual activities that exist in rugby – more often than not, with the lower divisions of Welsh rugby.

The Yard of Ale

I have not done the research, but I can guarantee that every clubhouse in Wales has the Yard of Ale, or at least has had it, but unfortunately, it has been smashed or broken. Go into any club in Wales and ask for a 'Yard' and the bar staff will look at you with a dumbfounded glance. For those who know little about the 'Yard', it is basically a long glass, which holds around three pints and has a bubble on the end. Quite normal, you might think. However, these drinking utensils are normally brought out for special occasions, such as festive gatherings and birthdays. Some rugby fanatics see it as a party piece for the most outrageous drinkers who have a degree in alcohol studies.

I was introduced to the 'Yard' whilst playing for the under-16s rugby team. It was during one of the internationals, when one of the 'big' drinkers took to the stage and downed the drink in less than three seconds. Memories of that evening are still rooted in my mind, and so too is the euphoric look on the drinker's face as he sidled back to his pint and his proud friends.

These days, the 'Yard' still comes out. However,

I have yet to see anyone beat the record I witnessed as a young lad; somehow, I don't think it will ever be emulated.

The Boxing Day Match

An unusual activity for me was always the Boxing Day match. For many clubs around Wales this was, and in some clubs still is, a time for the club's present side to take on the club's past. In some ways this is a good idea. However, having it on Boxing Day is, for me personally, a bit on the silly side. My reasons are quite palpable. First of all, it is bloody freezing on Boxing Day, and if the pitches are not frozen solid, you can bet yourself that it will be pissing down.

Second, if these games are to be organised, then organisation skills should be shown. For example, rugby is played with 15-a-side. On Boxing Day, this number increases slightly, and sometimes, if you're still a present player, you can find yourself playing against a team of 28. The ref (who is usually someone from the club and probably someone who hasn't reffed for about twenty years) simply doesn't say anything to the past players, purely because they resemble a pile of Neanderthals.

Third, my reason for calling the match 'unusual' is simply because of the timing of the meeting. Personally, having the game the day after Christmas Day is just not conducive to action for many players.

It might just be me, but playing a game a day after I've eaten half a farm, a bag of spuds, Aunt Bessie's favourites, and drunk about three kegs of lager just isn't the appropriate time for chasing a rugby ball about the place.

The last reason alludes, again, to organisation. Sides have to adhere to the time of kick-off, for 'normal' matches. However, Boxing Day matches are not 'normal' games, are they? And the club committee honestly think they can arrange kick-off for 11.00 a.m. on Boxing Day morning. This, unfortunately, is never the case, yet these clubs continue to stick with the festive fixture, despite the game kicking off at half-past two. 11.00 a.m. – it'll never happen.

Boxing Day matches can be great fun, I must admit. Watching some of the older players put on their kit is an amusing thing. Some of the boots I've seen worn would put Derek Quinnell's youth boots to shame, they honestly would. But some of these players haven't played for years and years: and you can tell this by the worn shorts; the 1970's socks with holes in the sole; headbands which went out of fashion when Mervyn Davies retired; and some players playing while wearing beards. Yes, it is great fun – but, let's face it, Boxing Day matches are slightly unusual. The fans might think it's a good idea and they probably do get a lot out of it. As for the past players, all they get out of it is a bout of heartburn, and a walking style like John Wayne for about three weeks after.

Kangaroo Court

Kangaroo Court, despite being unusual, is great fun if you are having a good knees-up, or if you're away on tour. From talking to people in clubs, I've heard some of the most bizarre stories involving club fans and players. I have witnessed the vilest of acts, acts that even Ant and Dec, in the jungle, would turn away from. There have been times when people have had to eat dog food sandwiches with tomato sauce, rotten fish and pickles, cat food kebabs etc. These punishments are given out because a certain player might have broken the rules during that particular season. These rules might be forgetting to wear a shirt and tie after a game; using your mobile to ring your missus in the changing room; refusing to sing, and so on. Personally, being a dedicated follower of the singing trade, I think a good cat food kebab is an apt punishment for refusing to sing.

One story I've heard that showed the callousness of the kangaroo court happened a few years back. The player who was to be punished, amazingly, wasn't a drinker – and that was the reason for the punishment. Showing absolutely no sympathy at all, the kangaroo court judges issued him his penalty, which was to neck back three pints of cider. Being a non-drinker, and worried about the fact that he had a bladder problem after too much drink, the player desperately tried to swap the punishment for another. He even pleaded for the dog food sandwich.

Despite his efforts, his pleas fell on deaf ears and the player had to down the cider. Fair play to him, he did do it. However, the state he was in a few hours later is a different story. Sporting no eyebrows and fringe (which had obviously been hacked off – another tour requirement) the boy was also saturated in some sort of fetid liquid.

Needless to say, the boy was left there to sleep it off; though the club did have an angry phone call from the boy's mother, who wasn't happy after having to wake up to a wet carpet in the front living room. And it wasn't water. Wink, wink!

Unusual things do happen in rugby clubs. Go down to the one nearest one to you. I guarantee you'll see something 'unusual' as you go in.

V – Valley people

I have met many valley people in my life; the main reason for this is that I live in the valleys. Every one that I've met has that sense of humour that you can associate with the valleys, and, for the letter V, I am going to mention a few characters that I've happened to meet during my rugby life.

To appreciate this kind of life, you would have to come here for yourself. Fortunately for me, I was brought up here, so it's fair to say that I've heard some stories.

The first tale is about a boy who used to play for a team called Penallta. It was the youth team and the boys were doing well that year. Having qualified for the Welsh Cup, every player had to be registered, in order to play in the games. As well as this, the WRU wanted a passport photo done for each player, really to make sure that everyone was the legal age to play in the youth team. Playing in the Welsh Cup was a lot different to the Rhymney Valley Cup. First rule was: if you were 27, you were too old.

Anyway, passport photos were needed. After a few weeks, everyone had had their photo done, except for this particular player. His excuse was that he was too busy working. After hours of asking, and stressing how important it was, the boy, clearly fed-up, slammed his fists on the table and said:

"Look, I'm busy working all week, but my mother's off work on Monday. I'll ask her to get my photo."

Unbelievable. The boy in question hadn't even realised what he had said. He still hasn't lived it down.

Another story is about a Valley Boy. This young man was on his driving test and was doing quite well. In those days, the driving tests were different from those of today. Nowadays, you have to pay to have a theory test and pay to have a driving test. Going back a few years, it was different, because the whole test was done on the same day. Critics have argued that it was easier in the old days, and cheaper. This boy obviously didn't mind either way. Happily driving across some country road, the examiner asked him what was the last sign they passed. Grinning slightly, and obviously confident about his answer, the trainee driver answered:

"Pick your own strawberries – two tubs for a pound."

He went on to fail the test, after getting the theory side of it wrong. The examiner was convinced he was taking the piss, when he asked what the next sign meant, wanting the correct answer: "Low Bridge." The proud driver said, "Caerphilly, 3 miles." He is now a taxi driver.

So, that's just two little anecdotes of life in the valleys. Both were good, strong rugby players. They just couldn't help being a bit dim.

W – Winning and Losing

The old saying: "No matter if you win or lose, it's the taking part that counts,' makes me wonder if it means anything at all. I believe it does hold some value because, after all, we can't all be winners, and some pride must be held for all those who take part in a game. However, if you really think about this saying, then most would think, "What a load of crap!" because everyone wants to win, and nobody wants to lose.

Picture the scenario now, if you're part of a rugby team that is having a trouncing every week. Do you really think that they come off the paddock and say to one another:

"It don't matter boys, it's the taking part that counts. Just think of next week, Swansea away. Could be another whitewash for us." Personally, I don't think they do. I think the conversation goes more along the lines of this:

"Jesus, boys, 123-0. We can't go on like this, mun. Look at us – a bare 15, and we've got John on the wing, who retired back in '83, and the bus driver on the other. Let's call it a day, boys."

Just to add to this assumption that winning is better, let's look at the night life in Cardiff, after a Wales win. You cannot beat the atmosphere. As you walk through the city, there is a sea of red, as fans celebrate the Welsh win. Losing, however, puts you on an immediate downer. Clubs and pubs are still relatively full, but it seems that no one wants to really party. After all, Wales have lost.

You can make the analogy that it's the same when people sit exams. I bet nearly everybody has been in the situation when they've been waiting for the results of some examination. Nervous? Anxious? Worried? These are the words that you can associate with that waiting. Then, when you eventually get the results you've been hoping for, how much of a relief is it? You can't describe the emotions. However, if you fail, you feel as though you've let yourself down. And you can almost gaurantee that someone from your family will take the piss out of you, and call you thick, despite the fact that he or she knows how low you feel.

Some people do not have to wait and suffer like others. An old player from my club knew from the start that he'd failed, because he turned up for an exam after having revised for a History examination, little knowing that on that particular day was GCSE Maths. He hadn't even taken his calculator!

People, as they read this, might be thinking that this is a little harsh. And in some ways it is. If you look at the world of sport, there are many people who participate because they simply enjoy it – and I accept that. On the other hand, being on the losing side – in which I have been quite a few times – is totally different to being on a winning one. Winning, to me, is everything.

To get a better, more lucid idea of this, focus your

minds back to the Grand Slam, back in 2005. That year, Wales played the best rugby in years, emulating our unbeatable side of the 70s. Beating England in the first game wasn't enough for the Welsh side. In their hearts, they believed that they had the potential to win the Grand Slam. And that is exactly what they did.

A year later, this winning streak soon came to an end; Wales simply couldn't retain their winning Grand Slam rugby. Fans were downtrodden, gutted at the fact that Wales only won a few of the matches.

The old saying: "It's not the winning, it's the taking part," certainly didn't wash with us fans and players. In Wales, it was simply obvious how much winning meant.

X – Xenophobia

As we are all aware, there is quite a bit of friction between the Welsh and the English, hence the reason why xenophobia has been allocated an entry into my book.

It would be unfair to say that the Welsh totally dislike the English 100%, because this would simply be untrue. The figure is probably around 99%, rather than the 100 mark. But seriously, most English people are sound and many a laugh has been had with them.

However, the English rugby team is entirely different. For some unknown reason, the Welsh despise the English rugby team. In fact, I think I'm right in saying that all the other teams involved in the Six Nations despise them, too. There are two teams I support in rugby: Wales – and anyone who is playing against England.

Being an enemy of the English rugby team has been a hobby in Wales for many years. I put it down to their total arrogance and belief that they are the greatest team in the world. Yes, they won the World Cup. But that was nearly 4 years ago, and English people are still harping on about it. To put it bluntly, you're as only as good as your last game. And we all know the English haven't been playing as well lately.

The English have got a slight argument, though, because Wales have been on the losing end to England on most occasions. So it would be a fair point to say that England is the better team. But, if you go back to the matches during the 70s, the results differed quite considerably. Due to this, the English were not so keen to label the Welsh team bad, because, nearly 100% of the time, they were on the losing side.

Over the years, things changed, and being on the beaten side against England seemed to piss off the Welsh even more. Famous English songs were polluted by the Welsh fans, and many of the lyrics often changed. Most fans and players in Wales now could easily tell the English where 'to stick their 'chariot'. The new version of that song – which I won't write down in this book – I much prefer to the old, duller one. It tends to give it more 'emphasis'.

The hostility towards the English grew so much that even Welsh bands started singing about the old enemy. The Stereophonics' song, 'As long as we beat the English', was an instant classic, and if it had been released in a Welsh-only chart, would have gone straight to number 1. It epitomised the feelings of the Welsh fans towards the English. Of course we wanted to win every one of our matches, but if we didn't, as long as we beat the English, we couldn't really care. They were our number 1 target.

One mean rugby lad takes a particular dislike to the English rugby team. Born of quite hardened parents and family, the boy was taught to fend for himself at quite a young age. Apparently, his father was so hard on the youngster that he bought him a swing and put it against the wall, and when he had troubles wetting the bed, bought him an electric blanket. Personally, though, I put these down to vicious rumours!

Looking back, the boy did have a good upbringing – even though it was hard. The time we spent in Magaluf, when he made his famous speech, will always remain rooted in my memory. After having an argument over rugby with some English fans, the boy stood up on the chair and said, "I love the Welsh, I love the Scottish and I love the Irish, but do you know what I think about the English?" With everyone too scared to answer, he whipped down his trousers and said, "I think they're pants." Funnily enough, the English were lost for words.

So X, for me, has to stand for Xenophobia. The tensions between Welsh and English rugby will continue for years to come; and, hopefully, it will provide some more entertaining songs for us Welsh to sing. The English will just love this.

Y – Years from now

Now that we're nearing the end of this amusing book on Welsh Rugby, I think it's time to look at the future. We have looked long and hard at the nature of our nation's favourite sport, concentrating closely on the wackier side of rugby in Wales, especially the tours. Being avid Welsh fans and players, everybody should know, if they didn't before, what being on tour involves. However, in the future, will these jaunts away still be the same? Will these tours still be the highlight of the rugby season – a time when the most respectable of team members show the darker sides of their personalities?

Also, what will happen in Welsh rugby? Will our nation be the best in the world? Will we beat teams like New Zealand and Australia, and will we be known as the greatest side in the British Isles? With the World Cup not that long away, these questions will be the main topics for discussion in clubs throughout the country, because the World Cup is such a massive honour in which to be involved.

These are questions that nobody can answer – because nobody can predict the future.

However, years from now, certain things, I believe, will still be the same, and one such is our love of rugby. Whether our national side is a team of wannabe Chippendales, or long-haired, bearded folk with headbands, fans will still go and watch. There will be great similarities at home matches, when 70,000 or more fans waltz through the city of Cardiff. Pubs will still be packed full to the rafters as bouncers let in twenty at a time. Fans will still be queuing twelve-deep at the bar to get a pint, tipping half of it as they try to squeeze through the gaps of sweating people. The Millennium Stadium will still be one of the greatest in the world, and will still have fourteen-mile queues to the bars and toilets at half-time.

But will this matter to the fans? The hustle and bustle is something that they put up with. The two-hour wait for a taxi to get home after the game will still be a part of the crack, so will having to squeeze on to a Rhymney Valley train carriage, while 2000 other people try and do the same. It is something that, to be a fervent Welsh rugby fan, you have put up with. Years from now, Wales will never lose its culture or its pride, and Welsh Rugby will never lose its fans.

Z – Zzzzzzzzz

I thought it quite apt to end this book with something that we associate with sleeping. It is quite hard to think of something that could relate to the letter Z. Don't get me wrong, I did think of something, but I didn't think it would suit the soothing tone of this book. As a result, then, I decided to use a reference to sleeping to end this book.

As I've said at the beginning, when someone goes on a rugby tour, especially if they are from Wales, sleep is almost non-existent. This changes when they arrive home, though, even for the hardened drinkers on tour.

When the coach arrives back at the rugby club of that particular club, many boys will stay out, 'just to round off' the tour. Some, on the other hand, will head straight for home, where they will, no doubt, fall immediately asleep.

But it doesn't matter if you stay out for that last day, or if you go straight home to bed. The bottom line is, no matter how much you can drink, or how much you can stay asleep while on tour, when you return to your beds, the inevitable happens – you fall asleep. And no matter how long you sleep, you still feel tired. You get up and you fall back to sleep. The pattern of snoozing takes you back to when you were a baby, sleeping in your mother's arms.

And this pattern will last for weeks, depending on what kind of tourist you are. For me, it can take ages. And that's why I've ended my book with this, because there is nothing better than your bed, when you return from a tour.

Don't believe me. Try four days on the piss with my rugby club, and you'll see.

I'm off now because I'm tired.

Zzzzzzzzzzzzzzzzzzzz.

* I can say, with total honesty, that all of the stories mentioned in this book are true. If you don't believe me, ask my mother.

I'm a rugby player – would I lie?!

Welsh Valleys Characters

David Jandrell

Welcome to the world of the Welsh valleys characters. Enjoy this delightful introduction to these real characters – their haunts, habits and humour.

£3.95 ISBN: 0 86243 772 5

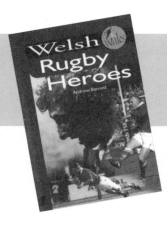

Welsh Rugby Heroes

Androw Bennett

£3.95 ISBN: 0 86243 772 5

Welsh Valleys Humour

David Jandrell

A first-time visitor to the south Wales Valleys will be subjected to a language that will initially be unfamiliar to them. This book features a tongue-in-cheek guide to the curious ways in which Valleys inhabitants use English, together with anecdotes, jokes, stories depicting Valleys life, and malapropisms from real-life Valleys situations!

"What a delight David Jandrell's book is!"
– **Ronnie Barker**

£3.95

ISBN: 0 86243 736 9

A–Z of Welsh Rugby is just one of
a whole range of Welsh-interest
publications from Y Lolfa. For a full list
of books currently in print, send now
for your free copy of our new, full colour
catalogue. Or simply surf into our website

www.ylolfa.com

for secure on-line ordering.

TALYBONT CEREDIGION CYMRU SY24 5AP
e-bost ylolfa@ylolfa.com
gwefan www.ylolfa.com
ffôn (01970) 832 304
ffacs 832 782